D1708537

EXERCISE AND FITNESS

Brian R. Ward

Series consultant:
Dr Alan Maryon-Davis
MB, BChir, MSc, MRCP, FFCM

CLINTON MIDDLE
SCHOOL LIBRARY

LIFE GUIDES

Franklin Watts
London · New York · Toronto · Sydney

© 1988 Franklin Watts

First published in 1988 by
Franklin Watts
12a Golden Square
London W1

First published in the USA by
Franklin Watts Inc.
387 Park Avenue South
New York, N.Y. 10016

First published in Australia by
Franklin Watts Australia
14 Mars Road
Lane Cove
New South Wales 2066

UK ISBN: 0 86313 667 2
US ISBN: 0-531-10562-8
Library of Congress Catalog Card No: 87-51697

Design: Howard Dyke

Picture research: Anne-Marie Ehrlich

Illustrations: Andrew Aloof, John Bavosi, Dick
Bonson, Penny Dann, Howard Dyke, Sally Launder,
David Mallott

The exercises on pages 40−44 are based on the Health
Education Authority's booklet *Exercise: Why Bother?*

Photographs:
Colorsport 17, 30*c*, 30*r*, 31*l*, 31*c*
Howard Dyke 11*b*, 45
Sally & Richard Greenhill 14, 29*b*
Impact Photos 11*t*, 36, 37
Sporting Pictures 12, 15
Tropix 31*r*
ZEFA 5, 7, 29*t*, 30*l*, 33

Printed in Belgium

Contents

Looking good and feeling good

Why do you need to take exercise? And what are the benefits of feeling fit? The two go together. Without exercise, you certainly won't either feel or be fit. And fitness is one of the foundations of good health.

Good health is not just the absence of illness. It is the combination of being physically fit and feeling good. There is no doubt that if you are feeling healthy you will be happier and more confident and able to cope better with school and other activities.

Regular exercise is the best way of keeping in shape. It helps you to lose weight and stay slim, improving your figure and posture.

Exercise also helps to avoid stress. Stress is a problem that affects both young and old because of pressures at home or at work. During a session of vigorous exercise you take your mind off your everyday problems and afterwards you will be pleasantly relaxed. Another benefit is that you will sleep better and wake up feeling refreshed.

Exercise helps you feel good in mind and body. It's also a good way of making new friends and enjoying your spare time more.

What is fitness?

The body works more efficiently when it is fit and can operate at its peak. Fitness is a combination of three important things: **suppleness**, **strength** and **stamina**.

Suppleness allows you to bend and twist freely and stay more active as you get older. Strength is something you need all the time – to climb stairs, push, pull and lift things. Stamina gives your muscles staying power and stops you feeling tired. You can only be truly fit if you exercise regularly to develop each of these three things.

There are no short cuts to fitness. It doesn't have to cost much – it may even be free if you choose to exercise at home or go walking or running. What it does need is time, the right kind of exercise and some determination to keep yourself physically active.

Best of all, fitness is fun. The more you exercise, the easier it gets and the more you will enjoy it.

Opposite
There are many ways to exercise which will improve your general fitness. Competitive sports, leisure activities and exercise training can all contribute towards your overall health. You can exercise on your own or with a group, whichever you prefer.

6

The healthy body

When you exercise by running, dancing or swimming, you feel your heart pumping more strongly and faster than usual. The working muscles need more **oxygen** than usual, so your heart has to beat faster to pump more oxygen-rich blood to them. One of the benefits of regular exercise is that the heart becomes more efficient at pumping blood around the body.

With regular exercise, the chemicals in the blood change, allowing it to flow more freely and making it less likely to clot and block blood vessels. In particular, the level of harmful fatty substances in the blood is reduced. This is important, because fatty deposits can clog up the walls of the **arteries** as we get older, causing **heart attacks** and other health problems later on.

Other changes and improvements take place in our bodies. Muscles become larger and stronger, and the rope-like **tendons** and **ligaments** which join muscles and bones become much stronger. Muscles also become more efficient at using oxygen to perform work. Even the bones are strengthened with regular exercise.

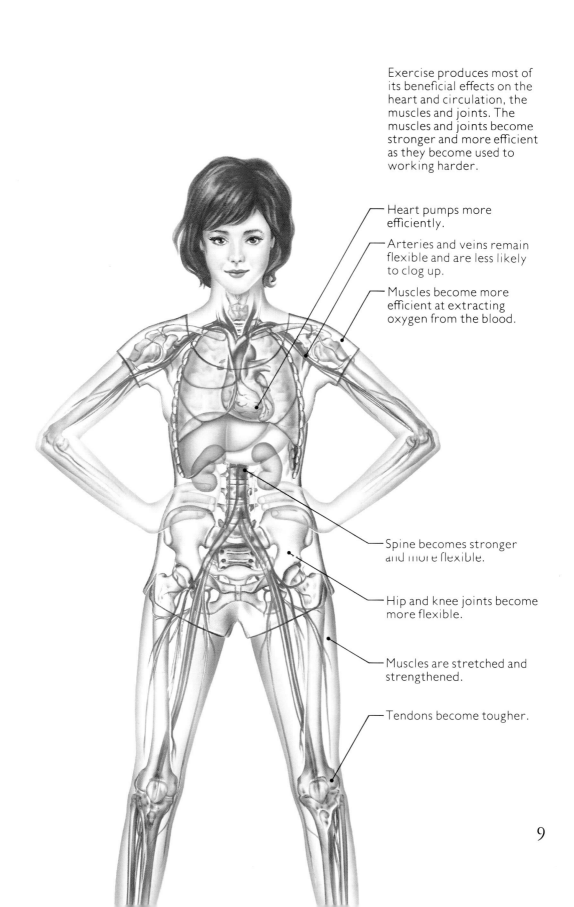

Exercise produces most of its beneficial effects on the heart and circulation, the muscles and joints. The muscles and joints become stronger and more efficient as they become used to working harder.

Heart pumps more efficiently.

Arteries and veins remain flexible and are less likely to clog up.

Muscles become more efficient at extracting oxygen from the blood.

Spine becomes stronger and more flexible.

Hip and knee joints become more flexible.

Muscles are stretched and strengthened.

Tendons become tougher.

9

Suppleness

Suppleness allows you to bend and twist freely, without strain or damage to the joints.
If you keep trying to touch your toes, the muscles in your back and legs gradually stretch so you can bend more freely.
An old person is much less supple than a healthy teenager, unless regular exercise has maintained flexibility.

One of the most important aspects of physical fitness is suppleness. This is the ability to bend and twist your body in any normal position, without too much effort, and without doing yourself any damage.

You need suppleness every day, for lifting, stretching, bending down – even when you first sit up in bed in the morning. The more supple you are, the less likely you are to hurt yourself in sports or in any other activity. **Sprains** and strains are less likely too. When you are supple, you can move faster and become more agile.

Suppleness is the result of regular exercise. The muscles that work the joint are gradually stretched, allowing the joint to bend farther. Muscles that are not regularly exercised gradually shorten, and the joints stiffen up. The results of exercise are most obvious in the back, which quickly becomes much more supple.

Many forms of exercise improve suppleness, especially yoga, swimming and dance. All these activities put extra demands on the joints and eventually make the whole body more supple.

◁ People who are truly fit put their suppleness to good use in their everyday activities. This woman finds it natural and convenient to perch her baby on her hip, taking advantage of the suppleness of her spine.

▷ Ballet and other forms of dance need suppleness as well as strength. Dancing is a good way to keep fit because it requires coordination to keep all parts of the body working together.

Strength

Males are generally stronger than females. This is partly because a greater proportion of the male body is made up of muscle. The diagram shows how grip strength in males becomes more powerful with increasing age, compared with that of girls.

Muscle strength is also an important part of fitness. Just like suppleness, strength helps to protect us from injury. Strong muscles support the joints, and help prevent sprains and strains. In your back, strong muscles improve posture by keeping the spine in its proper position. Firm muscles also keep your stomach tucked in.

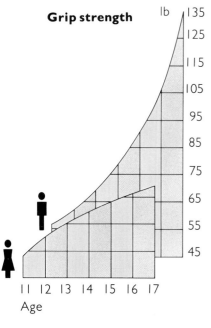

Grip strength

lb

135
125
115
105
95
85
75
65
55
45

11 12 13 14 15 16 17

Age

▷ Certain sports require a tremendous amount of strength. The tennis serve is an example where many of the body's muscles are used together for extra power.

The back is one of the most vulnerable parts of the body. It is often damaged when people pick up heavy objects by bending at the hip. This places all the strain on the back.

Use the strength of your leg muscles to help lift heavy objects. Squat down, keeping the back straight and nearly upright, so that the lifting power comes from the thigh muscles, the strongest in the body.

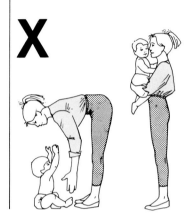 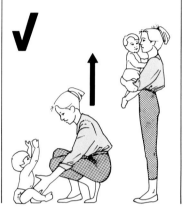

You need strength every time you stand up, lift or pull – even to support your own body's weight. Nearly half of your body weight is made up of muscle, and there are over 600 different muscles in the body. Muscles increase in size and strength quite quickly with regular exercise, and you can improve the strength of certain muscles by doing simple exercises like press-ups. But to become fit, all your muscles need regular exercise.

Developing strength does not mean producing muscles like a body builder. Strength alone is not true fitness. Training with weights is a very good way to improve muscular strength, but it needs to be combined with much more active forms of exercise.

Stamina

Walking or hiking for long distances, especially over uneven ground, can be an enjoyable and effective way of developing stamina.

Suppleness and strength are very important, but for true fitness, you also need to be able to continue to work or exercise for long periods without getting tired. Stamina is the third benefit you get from regular exercise, and is in many ways the most important.

With stamina you can walk or run without getting out of breath or tiring quickly, and it stops you feeling "worn out" when you carry out everyday activities. For most sports, stamina is vital if you are to keep up the pace.

Exercise to develop stamina produces changes in the muscles. The muscles become more efficient at extracting oxygen from the bloodstream and using it to power repetitive physical work.

To improve your stamina, you need to exercise hard, so that you become fairly breathless. You must keep stepping up your work load as you begin to build up stamina. Gradually, you will find that you no longer feel so out of breath. Continuous exercise, by running, swimming or walking, are all good ways to improve stamina, provided they are vigorous.

Being disabled is not necessarily a barrier to becoming fit. Many people confined to wheelchairs have developed strength and built up their stamina. Many enjoy sport, while some even take part in international competitions.

Aerobic energy

With regular exercise, your body gradually learns to use oxygen more efficiently. In this diagram, you can see that the improvement gradually levels off after weeks of training. After this, you still need to work hard enough to keep at this maximum figure.

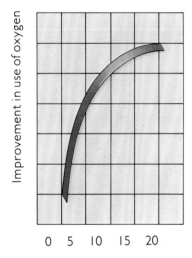

Weeks of exercise training

Opposite
In sports where short bursts of effort are needed, such as sprinting, the muscles can build up an "oxygen debt" when anaerobic activity takes place.

Our bodies depend on oxygen from the air we breathe to help break down substances from food to make energy. This energy powers all the processes that keep us alive, including muscle activity. Because normal exercise uses a lot of the oxygen we obtain from the air during breathing, it is called **aerobic** activity.

Some forms of very strenuous activity, like playing squash, use so much oxygen in a short time that the body cannot replace it quickly enough. For short periods the muscles can work in a different way, called **anaerobic** activity, but they tire very quickly and soon resume working in the normal aerobic way.

Oxygen is used to burn up sugars stored in the body, releasing energy in the form of **calories**. With exercise, various changes take place in the body helping us to use oxygen more efficiently. The blood becomes capable of carrying more oxygen, and the structure of the muscle changes so that it can use more oxygen. The result is improved stamina and greater strength, all contributing to better fitness.

Exercise and weight

Fat is stored under the skin, but in women, this fat layer is thicker than in men. Fat tends to build up in different places in the two sexes. In men it is stored mostly in the abdomen, while in women fat is stored in the buttocks, thighs and breasts.

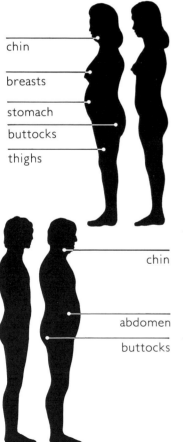

chin

breasts

stomach

buttocks

thighs

chin

abdomen

buttocks

Regular exercise consumes energy or calories produced from the food we eat. But if we do not get enough exercise, or if we eat too much, there will be energy or calories to spare. The body does not waste anything that could be useful, so it stores away the excess energy in the form of fat, which can be broken down again to produce energy when needed.

Normally the body consists of 10–20% fat, but if we become overweight, the percentage soon creeps up. Fat is stored under the skin and around the internal organs.

Many people are overweight, and for some, the results will eventually be poor health. They are more likely to damage hip and leg joints, because of the extra load they carry. Excess weight may even be a threat to life. It is known to increase the risk of **high blood pressure** and other diseases of the heart and circulatory system. **Diabetes** is also more common in overweight people.

The solution to all these problems is very simple. Eat a sensible diet, not too high in calories, and get plenty of exercise to burn off small amounts of excess calories.

Every time you eat a 100 g (4 oz) chocolate bar, you are taking in about 650 calories of extra energy. This may not sound much, but if it is surplus to your daily needs, it will be turned into fat – about 75 g (3 oz) per chocolate bar. And if you want to burn off this surplus energy, so it won't be turned into fat, you will have to do a surprising amount of extra exercise. The times given are for a young person weighing about 40 kg (88 lb). The times will be less for an adult woman or man.

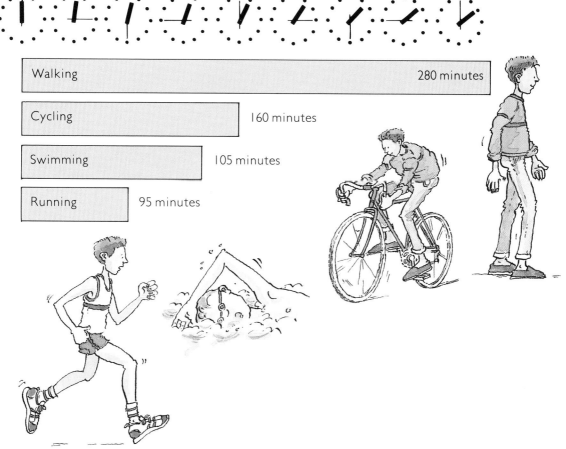

Walking	280 minutes
Cycling	160 minutes
Swimming	105 minutes
Running	95 minutes

Exercise and your heart

The healthy heart can cope with exercise by pumping more blood. The unfit heart has to beat faster to circulate enough oxygen.

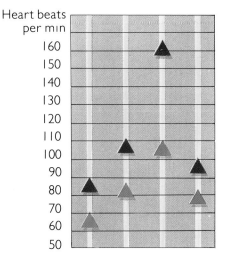

Heart beats per min

160
150
140
130
120
110
100
90
80
70
60
50

Resting   Standing   Climbing stairs   Sitting

▲ Unfit person
△ Fit person

The heart is a large muscular organ which pumps oxygen-rich blood around the body. Like any other muscle, it becomes stronger and more efficient if extra demands are put on it by regular vigorous exercise.

When you exercise, your body needs more oxygen, so the heart has to pump (or beat) faster to increase the blood flow. But a fit heart does not have to work as hard as an unfit heart because it is more efficient, pumping larger amounts of blood with each beat.

The radial artery runs just below the skin on the inside of the wrist, on the same side as the thumb. Because it is so near the surface, this artery can easily be felt and used to measure pulse rate.

Place the fingertips over the artery, and steady the hand by gently holding the thumb against the other side of the wrist. Now you can count the number of pulses in 15 seconds and multiply by four to give the pulse rate per minute.

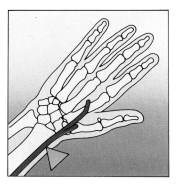

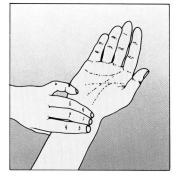

You can find out how efficiently your heart is working by checking your pulse rate before and after a small, standard amount of exercise. First you need to know how fast your heart beats normally. Check your resting pulse rate, before you do the exercise, and write it down.

Next, step up on to a stair, then step down again, moving one foot after the other. Repeat this 24 times a minute, for a total of 3 minutes. Immediately take your pulse. This is your exercise pulse rate.

Sit down for 30 seconds, and check your pulse again to record your recovery pulse rate. Now you have some pulse rates against which you can compare your performance after you have been exercising regularly.

In addition, the muscles become more efficient at extracting oxygen from the blood. As a result, the fit person does not need such a big increase in blood flow and the heart beats more slowly than that of an unfit person.

Your heart beat, or **pulse** rate, can be clearly felt with the fingertips where arteries run near the surface of the body. The pulse most easily found is on the inside of the wrist. It is a useful measure of your fitness to check your pulse rate before and after exercise, and to see how the rate improves when you carry out an exercise program.

Measuring your fitness

Keep a record of how fast you can run over a moderate distance. This will give you a rough guide to how fit (or unfit) you are. Repeat the test to see how your fitness improves with regular exercise.

Minutes taken to cover 1 mile

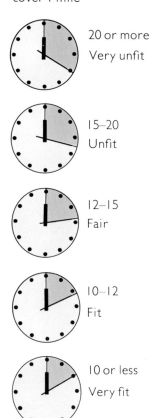

20 or more
Very unfit

15–20
Unfit

12–15
Fair

10–12
Fit

10 or less
Very fit

Once you start to exercise regularly, you will find some important changes in your pulse rate, which show how your fitness is improving. For example, an adult's normal resting pulse rate may be 65–75 beats per minute. But as fitness improves, together with the efficiency of the heart, the pulse rate can drop to 60 or less.

The fit person's heart will not need to work so hard during exercise, and will recover more rapidly afterwards. A person who is unfit may have a recovery pulse rate of 120 or more, while after exercise training this will probably fall to 80–90 beats per minute.

These benefits are easy to measure if you plan your exercise properly. First you must choose types of exercise that use as many of the larger muscles as possible, and that are rhythmic and aerobic, such as jogging or swimming. You will need to carry out the exercise at least twice a week, with a total exercise time each week of at least 60 minutes. While you are exercising, your pulse rate should be between 140 and 160 beats per minute. You should step up the exercise to maintain this figure as your heart gradually becomes more efficient.

Once you have started exercising regularly, you may want to check the rate at which your fitness improves. Work out a safe and traffic-free route of about 1500 m (1 mile). You can check the distance on a map, or get someone to measure it on the odometer of their car.

It will be more fun if you do the test with a friend. Put on comfortable clothes and running shoes before you set out. You may need to start with a mixture of running and walking at first. Go as fast as you can without getting too breathless. If you feel pain or discomfort, slow down or stop for a rest.

Make a note of the time you have taken to cover the distance or ask a friend to time you. You can judge your fitness by comparing your time against the chart shown opposite. Repeat the test in a month's time to check your progress and to encourage yourself to keep exercising.

23

Taking good care of your body

Your body is a complicated machine which can stand a surprising amount of wear and tear. But if you want to remain healthy throughout your life you must look after your body by avoiding things that can harm it. Smoking, stress or the wrong kind of diet can all lead to heart disease. Excessive drinking and drug taking can cause a variety of mental and physical problems. All these can cause lingering illness and threaten health or life itself.

Taking non-medical drugs is a sure way to damage your body, and probably also your mind. It's not the drugs alone that do the damage. Drug users tend to neglect their health and their diet, and those who inject drugs run the risk of catching dangerous infections, including AIDS.

Alcohol, except in small amounts, can destroy peak fitness and damage the body. Heavy drinkers risk damage to the liver and other organs. Alcohol is high in calories – another problem for people who are trying to keep fit.

Smoking is bad for health. The long-term risks are permanent lung or heart damage. If you are trying to keep fit, don't smoke. Smoking will make you breathless and wheezy. Tar deposited in the lungs makes you cough, and the blood is not able to carry oxygen efficiently.

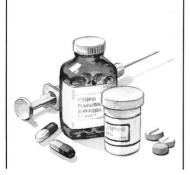

But another threat to your health is to do nothing at all. Lack of exercise, combined with some of the risk factors described and shown below, may result in general ill health or shorten life, usually through diseases of the heart and circulation.

Exercise is the best way to ensure that you stay healthy for as long as possible. All you need to do is invest a little time each week improving your fitness through exercise.

Stress is a result of continuous overwork, worry, or tension. It affects the mind and body, and can make you feel run down. You can fight stress with an exercise program which helps you to relax.

Although there is no truth in the old saying that you need 8 hours sleep every night, you must have adequate sleep. The amount each person needs varies. The best solution is to get enough sleep to feel rested and alert. Take a nap or sleep late to catch up if you have been missing out on sleep.

Lack of exercise can cause ill health. Your muscles get flabby and your heart becomes less efficient. Then when your muscles are called on, your heart pounds and your legs feel like rubber. Everyone needs to take some regular exercise to function well and to avoid serious health problems later in life.

Enjoying exercise

Exercise is fun, and there are many ways to enjoy it. In competitive sports you can get every conceivable form of exercise. But if you don't like to compete, there are just as many non-competitive ways to keep in shape.

The list of activities below shows there are many different ways of keeping fit. While it makes sense to choose a form of exercise that improves the three key factors of suppleness, strength and stamina, there are other things to think about as well.

ACTIVITY	Suppleness	Strength	Stamina	Sociability	Economy
Archery	**	**	*	**	**
Badminton	**	**	**	**	**
Baseball	**	**	**	***	**
Basketball	**	**	***	**	**
Bowling	*	*	*	**	**
Boxing	**	***	***	*	**
Canoeing	**	***	**	**	*
Cycling	*	***	***	**	**
Dancing (disco)	***	***	**	***	***
Fencing	***	***	**	**	**
Football	**	***	**	*	**
Golf	**	*	*	**	*
Gymnastics	***	***	*	**	**
Hiking	**	**	***	**	***
Hockey (field)	**	**	**	**	***
Hockey (ice)	***	***	***	**	*
Horse riding	*	**	*	**	*
Judo/karate	***	**	*	**	***
Mountaineering	**	***	**	**	**
Orienteering	*	**	***	**	***
Rowing	*	***	***	***	**

You may choose a sport that brings you in contact with lots of other people, so you make new friends. You may like more solitary outdoor pursuits like orienteering, or you might prefer to exercise in small groups, climbing or cycling.

You are going to spend quite a lot of time carrying out your exercise program, so choose activities that won't leave you bored after a few weeks – a mixture of different types of activity is probably best.

*** The more stars the better

ACTIVITY	Suppleness	Strength	Stamina	Sociability	Economy
Running	*	***	***	*	***
Sailing	*	**	*	**	*
Skating (ice)	***	**	***	**	**
Skating (roller)	***	**	**	**	***
Skiing (downhill)	***	***	**	***	*
Skipping	*	**	***	*	***
Soccer	**	***	**	**	***
Squash	***	**	**	**	**
Surfing	**	**	*	**	**
Swimming	***	***	***	*	***
Table tennis	**	*	**	**	***
Tennis	**	***	**	**	**
Volleyball	**	***	**	**	***
Walking	*	*	**	*	***
Water skiing	*	**	**	**	*
Weight lifting	**	***	*	**	**

Outdoor pursuits

Outdoor exercise is one of the cheapest ways to get fit and stay fit. The type of activity you take up will depend largely on where you live.

You can run or jog almost anywhere, but if you live in a crowded city it may be safer and more fun if you jog in a local park or recreation ground.

Walking is the easiest form of exercise, but to improve fitness, it should exert you enough to make you slightly breathless and to increase your pulse rate. This means a long, brisk walk, not just a comfortable stroll.

Bicycling is extremely good for developing stamina and strength, but usually only the muscles of the back and legs benefit. Again it is important to keep the pace up, and this usually means extra care about road safety.

Of all types of exercise, swimming is probably the best in terms of the three key factors of suppleness, strength and stamina. And unlike many other types of exercise, you are unlikely to strain yourself by overdoing things in the early stages because your body is supported by the water.

Jogging is good for developing stamina, but is less effective in improving strength and suppleness. You don't have to jog on your own. Organized runs allow you to take part in an event without going in for serious competitive running.

Swimming is one of the best all-round forms of exercise, provided you swim for long enough. Vary your stroke occasionally to make sure that all your muscles are used.

School sports

Taking part in active sport is an enjoyable and challenging way to exercise, although the benefits depend on the type of sport involved. Team games are a popular form of exercise in schools, and they can be an important part of a fitness program. But it is important to realize that not all team games provide the *constant* levels of aerobic exercise that are essential for improving stamina. You will need to be fairly breathless for at least 20 minutes to get real benefit.

Cycling is a very good aerobic exercise for developing stamina and strength. Because little of the body moves apart from the legs, it does not develop suppleness throughout the body.

Field hockey is a tough game which can be played by girls or boys. It demands a lot of running, so stamina is built up, together with strength in the legs and shoulders.

Canoeing is a very demanding pastime, which develops considerable strength and stamina, especially in the arms and shoulders.

CLINTON MIDDLE
SCHOOL LIBRARY

Many team games need short bursts of exercise, rather than continuous effort. Tennis, squash and basketball are ideal, because they require stamina, strength, and constant agile movement, while table tennis depends more on speed and agility.

Sports can have the disadvantage that injury is relatively common, but with proper coaching, this should not put anyone off from using sports to improve their overall fitness.

In soccer, strength is more important than suppleness or stamina. Players usually run for only short distances, so stamina is not built up on the field.

Stamina and strength are very important for the cross-country runner, although suppleness is less critical. Running on rough ground is much harder than track running.

Volleyball is a surprisingly strenuous sport, and because of its continuous speed, is very good for developing stamina.

Exercise classes

Attending exercise classes is probably the most social way to keep fit, and for many people, this element is as important as the actual exercise.

Most indoor leisure activities improve suppleness and stamina rather than strength, so some additional type of exercise will also be needed in order to become truly fit.

Yoga is a popular form of physical and mental discipline which makes the joints very supple. It is also a good way to learn to relax. However, it has almost no beneficial effects on the heart and circulation, because it requires little physical exertion.

Dance exercise, or aerobic exercise to music, improves both suppleness and stamina, because it involves strenuous movement for long periods.

Martial arts such as judo and karate involve the use of physical strength as well as suppleness and stamina, so they are particularly good for improving fitness. They require the combination of all these factors with speed and physical coordination, so they are a good basis for a fitness program.

Aerobic dancing to music is a popular way to keep fit. The proper combination of exercises can improve strength as well as suppleness and stamina.

Working out

Working out indoors doesn't depend on the weather. You can train at home very easily and cheaply and build up a reasonable level of fitness.

A good way to improve your fitness is to join a local health club or gymnasium. You will have the advantage of an instructor to show you what to do, and to monitor your progress. Some of the apparatus used in gymnasiums is very simple, and could be improvised at home. The more complicated exercise machines need careful supervision if you are to get the best out of them and avoid overstraining yourself in the early stages. You can train in any way you want, to develop suppleness, strength and stamina, but the use of these facilities can sometimes be expensive.

Working out with weights can be done at home or in a gym. This is a very efficient way to improve fitness in all respects, and should not be confused with weight *lifting*, which simply develops huge muscles, without any particular benefits for stamina or suppleness.

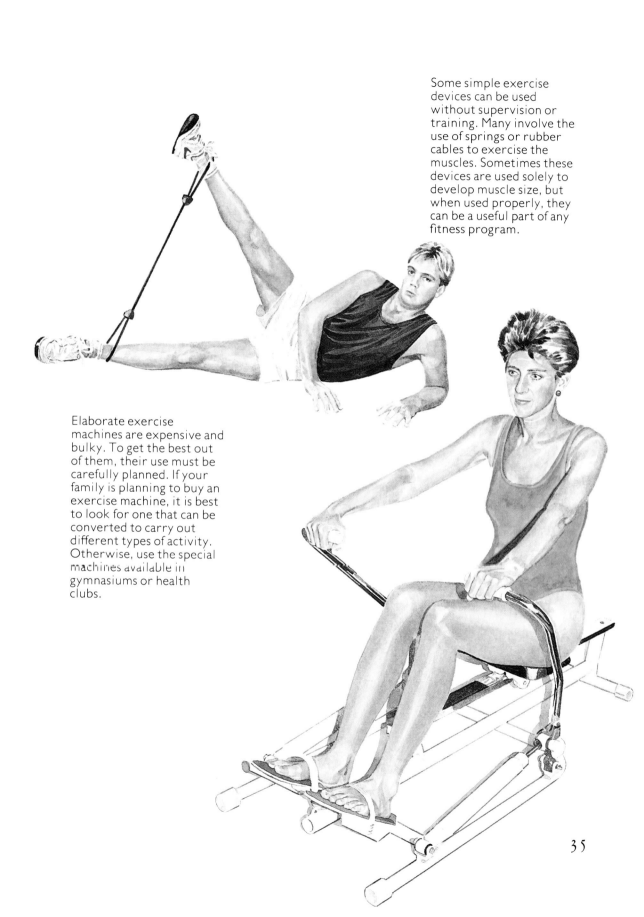

Some simple exercise devices can be used without supervision or training. Many involve the use of springs or rubber cables to exercise the muscles. Sometimes these devices are used solely to develop muscle size, but when used properly, they can be a useful part of any fitness program.

Elaborate exercise machines are expensive and bulky. To get the best out of them, their use must be carefully planned. If your family is planning to buy an exercise machine, it is best to look for one that can be converted to carry out different types of activity. Otherwise, use the special machines available in gymnasiums or health clubs.

Warming up

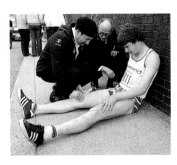

Muscle **cramps** occur when you have been working too hard, and muscles cannot cope any more. Waste products build up in the muscles and cause a sharp pain, which is a warning to rest for a while.

Even when you are fit, your body needs to prepare itself with warming-up exercises. These are intended to get the stiffness out of your joints and muscles before you begin exercising in earnest.

You should *never* exercise so hard that it becomes painful – just sufficiently to become a little hot and breathless, and to get your heart working harder. If you push yourself too hard in the early stages, you may damage the ligaments in your joints, or tear a muscle.

At the end of a period of exercise it is just as important to wind down gradually. Your body has been working overtime, and your heart pumping very hard while you were exercising. If you continue to exercise gently for a while, you give your body time to settle down.

After exercise, it is particularly important to put on warm clothes, even though you may feel very hot and sweaty. Your body has been trying to get rid of the heat produced when energy is released to power the muscles. Because this process continues for a while after exercise, you can easily become chilled unless you put on warm clothes.

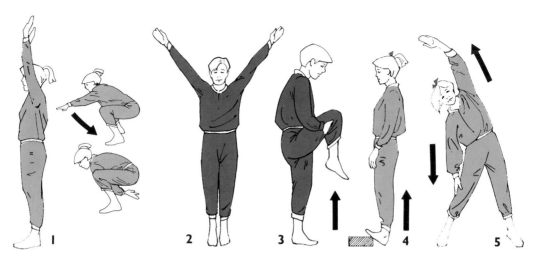

Here are some warming-up and cooling-down exercises.
1 Stretch your arms above your head, then bend your legs and swing your arms down and back behind you. Repeat 5 times.

2 Loosen the shoulders by swinging the arms first forwards, then back. Repeat 5 times.
3 Exercise knees, thighs and hips by pulling each knee in turn into your chest. Repeat 5 times.

4 Calf muscles benefit from the curb drop. Press up on to your toes, then drop slowly back on to your heels. Repeat 5 times.
5 Stretch the waist by bending as shown, 5 times in each direction.

It is important to prevent temperature drop after prolonged exercise. These marathon runners have been given insulating foil blankets to conserve heat, but you can use a sweater or track-suit top.

The right clothing

Don't try to save money with cheap footwear if you are going to run or jog. Good shoes should last you for hundreds of miles. If you are running on sidewalks or roads, you should buy shoes with deep, soft treads on the sole to absorb the impact as your foot strikes the ground. On grass or soft tracks, shallower treads are suitable. You must also make sure that the shoe bends freely at the ball of the foot, not under the arch.

Whatever type of exercise you try, it will be more pleasant and effective if you are wearing the proper clothing. This doesn't have to be expensive, but it should allow you to move freely and keep you warm. A T-shirt and shorts may be all you need in warm weather, but a track suit is better when it is cool. Remember that loose-fitting, natural cotton clothing is cooler and more comfortable than artificial fibers.

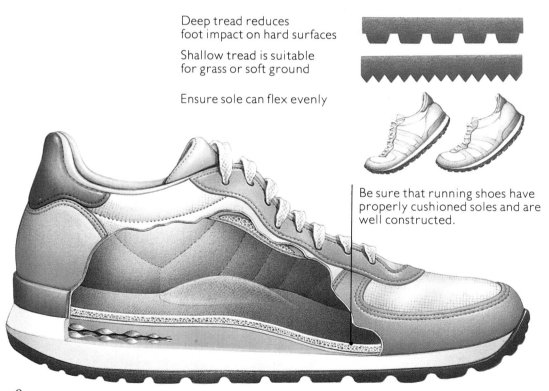

Deep tread reduces foot impact on hard surfaces

Shallow tread is suitable for grass or soft ground

Ensure sole can flex evenly

Be sure that running shoes have properly cushioned soles and are well constructed.

The proper footwear is very important. Pounding along roads or footpaths with ordinary tennis shoes will soon bruise your feet and cause blisters. The right type of training or running shoes will cushion and protect your feet, so get the proper footwear.

Special clothing and equipment may be needed for certain types of outdoor activities. For some you'll need weatherproof clothing to prevent exposure, while for others you'll need protection from the sun. Jeans are seldom satisfactory in bad weather. Wet jeans take a long time to dry out and are no protection from the cold. For some of the more specialized activities such climbing or canoeing, you must have the proper equipment, and this will be recommended by your instructor.

The ideal clothing for exercise allows you to move easily while keeping you warm and protecting you from extremes of weather. Running is much easier when you are wearing shorts rather than heavy or tight jeans which restrict movement. It may be sensible to tie a track-suit top loosely around your shoulders or waist in case it rains. Similarly, you may need protection from the sun.

Exercises for suppleness

Exercising at home is convenient, and for those who are self-conscious about their lack of fitness, it is private. You can soon build up to a satisfactory level of fitness before joining a club or class.

The following stretching exercises will all improve your suppleness.

Arm circling is a good way to improve the suppleness of your shoulders. Place your right hand on your right shoulder. Move your elbow forward, up and back in a circle. Then repeat with the other arm. Continue with alternate arms. Now swing your whole straight arm forward, up and back, first on alternate sides and then together.

Forward bending helps your shoulders, trunk and legs. First stretch up as far as you can, then bend forward at the knees and hips, as low as you can go. Straighten up and stretch up again, repeating the process.

The back muscles are stretched by side bending. Place feet apart, then bend slowly to one side, from the waist, sliding the hand down the outside of the thigh. Make sure you bend sideways and don't let your shoulders drop forward. Repeat for each side alternately.

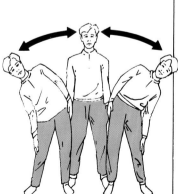

The exercises should be performed slowly, without forcing them. Try to do them at least 3 times a week and repeat each movement 8–12 times. These exercises are also useful for warming up before an exercise session.

This exercise stretches your thigh muscles and loosens the hip joint. Support your weight on your left leg and rest your left hand on the back of a chair for balance. Swing your right leg forward and backward as far as you can go, keeping your body upright. Repeat with the other leg.

To stretch the calf muscles and ankles, stand at arms' length from the wall and place your hands on the wall, as shown. Stretch one leg out behind you, with the ball of your foot on the floor and toes pointing towards the wall. Push the heel of this foot down to the floor, bending the other leg at the knee if necessary. Repeat with the other leg.

This exercise stretches the lower back and thigh muscles. Sit on the floor with your legs stretched straight out in front of you. Place your hands on your thighs and slowly slide your hands down your legs as far as is comfortable. Return to the upright position and repeat.

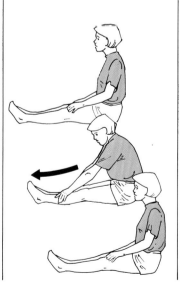

Exercises for strength

Developing your strength at home does not mean body-building exercises, neither does it mean long and painful exercise. You can begin to develop your strength by repeating the exercises shown five or six times at each exercise session, building up gradually into 20 repeats when you become really fit.

There are several exercises to develop the muscles of the arms and shoulders. Standing press-ups are quite easy to start with. Stand at arms' length from a wall and place your hands on the wall with your arms straight. Bend your arms until your forehead touches the wall. Then push yourself away until your arms are straight.

Press-ups are slightly harder from a kneeling position. For this exercise, you must take most of your weight on your arms, lowering the upper part of your body towards the floor as the arms bend, then pushing yourself back to the original position. Don't let your back sag in the middle.

Once you are feeling stronger, you can try the full press-up. This time, you must keep your whole body straight, lowering yourself until your face touches the floor, then pushing yourself up until the arms are straight again.

Muscles in the back and abdomen also need strengthening. Lie on your back, with your knees raised, and your hands resting on the front of your thighs. Now lift your head and shoulders, reaching towards your knees as far as you can without being uncomfortable. Let yourself uncurl slowly, then repeat.

The chest lift helps to strengthen muscles in the back. Lie on your stomach with arms at your sides and your head turned to one side. Gradually lift your head, neck and shoulders from the floor, turning

your head so that you are looking at the floor. Keep your chin tucked in. Return gradually to the original position, but turn your head to the other side. Then repeat.

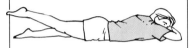

The leg lift helps to strengthen your hips and back. Lie on your stomach on the floor. Keeping your legs straight, raise one leg away from the floor as far as possible. Lower gently and repeat with the other leg.

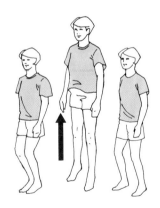

A vigorous exercise to improve both strength and stamina is the standing jump. Stand with your feet together and knees slightly bent. Spring up as high as you can, and land back with

your feet apart and knees bent. Now spring up again and land with your feet together. Repeat the exercise – apart, together, apart, together . . .

A much more vigorous exercise starts from the squatting position. In one smooth movement, you must uncoil yourself and spring up into the air, opening arms and legs like a starfish, before landing with the feet apart. Jump up again, closing the legs and dropping back into the squat position as you land. Repeat the exercise to build up stamina.

Exercises for stamina

Stamina-developing exercise (also called "aerobic" exercise) is an activity which makes you fairly breathless for at least 20 minutes at a time, at least twice a week. Stamina is a difficult thing to measure, unless you check your performance regularly using the performance chart shown on page 22 of this book. As you build up your stamina you will enjoy exercise more.

It is very simple, though perhaps rather boring, to build up stamina by carrying out simple repetitive exercises. Simply stepping up on to a stair, then down again, can improve stamina, provided it is repeated at length and regularly. You could also try running up and down stairs.

More enjoyable ways to improve stamina are simple activities such as skipping, which exercises a surprising number of muscles, or dancing, or running on the spot. Proper use of home exercise machines can develop stamina, along with strength and suppleness.

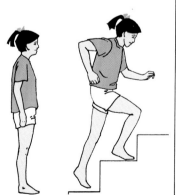

Glossary

Aerobic exercise: type of exercise in which the muscles use large amounts of oxygen. This means that the exercise must be sufficiently vigorous to make you breathless for some time.

Anaerobic exercise: exercise in which the muscles work for a short while without oxygen. This is typical of sports such as sprinting, which need immense effort for a very short time.

Artery: vessel carrying blood away from the heart, for distribution to other parts of the body.

Calories: units of measurement which are used to describe the amount of energy made available to the body from the food we eat.

Cramps: condition which can result from overuse of a muscle, in which the muscle contracts painfully. Muscle cramps are usually eased by massaging the muscle, and gently straightening the affected limb.

Diabetes: if the body does not produce enough of a substance called insulin, it cannot properly use sugar from our food, and a condition called diabetes results. It can be controlled by drugs or injections of insulin.

Heart attack: caused by blockage of an artery supplying blood to the heart muscle. This causes a lack of oxygen, and part of the heart muscle is damaged or dies.

High blood pressure: our blood must be under pressure to force it through the network of blood vessels and around the body. But if the pressure is too high, it can damage organs such as the heart, brain and kidneys.

Ligament: tough material which holds the bones of a joint together, while still allowing them to move freely.

Oxygen: colorless gas absorbed from the air into the blood during breathing. Large amounts of oxygen are needed for aerobic muscular activity.

Pulse: pumping action of the heart. The pulse can be felt with the fingertips where arteries are near the surface of the skin. The pulse rate can be measured, and is the number of heartbeats per minute.

Spine: bony support for the back. It is made up of many small bones called vertebrae.

Sprain: condition in which a joint is wrenched or twisted, or bent too far, or in the wrong direction. The soft tissues around the joint become damaged, and the whole joint is swollen and painful.

Stamina: the ability to continue exercising for a long time, without becoming too tired.

Strength: muscular power.

Suppleness: ability to bend and flex the body freely, without damaging the joints.

Tendon: tough rope-like strand, attached to the end of a muscle, and anchoring it to a bone, or to another muscle.

Vein: thin-walled blood vessel which returns blood to the heart.

Index